Introduction

This collection of 50 gifts to make yourself, to give to others, is not just for established crafters but for anyone with a love of all things beautiful. What you'll discover throughout is that the projects provide an opportunity to indulge your love of pattern and colour, making the simplest of gifts look sophisticated and elegant.

And, while experiencing the joy of choosing fabrics, yarns, patterned papers, ribbons and beads, you'll be trying your hand at a wide range of crafts, including knitting, papercraft, crochet, appliqué, sewing, beading, patchwork and quilting. All of the projects are ideal for those just getting started or with only basic skills, although some may stretch you – but they are well worth that extra effort. For experienced crafters the book offers 50 great ideas to adapt and enhance with your own specials skills.

Many of the projects take a couple of hours or less – some take only minutes – and all can be completed easily in a weekend, making them ideal for that last-minute gift or when you have a number to make, like at Christmas time. The Needle Know-how pages show the sewing, crochet and knitting skills you will need to complete the projects in a simple visual way. Templates for featured projects are provided at the back of the book and are also available at: http://ideas.sewandso.co.uk/patterns.

Nothing says 'I love you' more to friends and family than making time for them, so, whether you're a needle newbie or sewing sage, grab a cup of coffee, decide which project is just right for your loved one and get crafting this weekend!

ELLEN KHARADE

Gilded Vintage Frame

A junk-shop vintage picture frame is given a new lease of life by gilding with 9ct gold leaf. For a real vintage look, you could use it to display an old sepia photograph, maybe of some mysterious relatives with an untold story.

1. Using a wide bristle brush, apply a thin undercoat of acrylic primer paint to the frame and leave for several hours to dry out.

2. Using a wide dust-free bristle brush, apply a coating of gold-leaf size to the frame, making sure that it is completely covered. Leave the frame in a dust-free environment for at least 12 to 24 hours for the size to become tacky.

3. Carefully pick up the gold leaf using the corner of a paintbrush and gently lay it over the frame. Press the leaf onto the frame using the brush.

4. Continue in this way until the frame is completely covered, taking care not to miss out any areas. Stray bits of gold leaf can be picked up and re-applied to sized areas.

5. Once completed, gently brush with a large bristle brush to remove any stray bits of gold leaf.

6. Using a soft cloth or a large piece of cotton wool gently rub over the frame to burnish the leaf to a soft sheen and to make sure the gold has adhered well to the frame.

Gather
- Old junk-shop picture frame
- Acrylic primer paint
- Wide bristle brushes
- Paintbrush
- Gold-leaf size
- 9ct gold leaf, loose
- Soft, clean cloth

50 DIY *Gifts*

Fifty handmade gifts for creative giving

Edited by Ame Verso

www.sewandso.co.uk

Contents

LINDA CLEMENTS

Striped Lap Quilt

This quilt is easy to make for a special Mother's Day gift. You could add more strips to make it into a single-bed quilt. Why not try adapting the colour scheme for a Father's Day present?

1. Arrange the strips and sew them together along the long sides using 6mm (¼in) seams; press. Trim so the edges are straight.

2. Cut the wadding slightly larger and safety pin it to the back of the quilt, with the layers flat. Machine or hand quilt 1.3cm (½in) away from each seam. Remove the pins, press and trim the wadding so it is flush with the quilt.

3. Prepare the backing fabric so that it is 5cm (2in) larger than the quilt all around. Place the backing right side down and the quilt right side up on top, with a border of backing all round. Safety pin the layers together.

4. Do further quilting 1.3cm (½in) away from the previous quilting lines. Remove the pins and

press. Pull the quilting thread ends through to the front of the quilt.

5. Trim the backing so that it is 2.5cm (1in) larger than the quilt all round. Working one side at a time, fold the backing over by 1.3cm (½in) and then again, on to the quilt front. Pin in place and machine sew 3mm (⅛in) from the edge of the binding. Repeat on all sides and press.

Gather
- Five prints: 0.25m (¼yd) of each cut into two strips 12.7cm x 111.8cm (5in x 44in)
- White backing fabric 1.6m (1¾yd) 106.7cm (42in) wide
- Wadding (batting) 127cm (50in) square
- Sewing thread
- Quilting thread
- Safety pins

JENNIFER GRACE

Tissue Paper Flowers

These exotic tissue paper flowers with their jewel-bright beaded centres make pretty corsages and are also perfect for adding a flamboyant touch to wedding gifts. If you would like a more delicate look, choose papers in colours to complement the bride's and bridesmaids' dresses.

1. Cut 10 rectangles of tissue paper measuring 12cm x 18cm (4¾in x 7in). Lay the paper rectangles on top of each other to make a neat stack. Making sure a short edge is nearest to you, begin to concertina fold – fan style – making the folds approximately 1cm (⅜in) apart.

2. Cut a 5cm (2in) length of wire and twist it tightly around the middle of the tissue paper fan, folding the excess flat against the back of the flower. Cut the ends of the flattened fan into arch shapes. Unfold the flower to reveal the scalloped petals.

3. Gently lift the tissue paper layers to separate them, to give the flower some dimension, and pull them lightly to join the petal gaps (there is no need to glue them together).

4. Put a 2.5cm (1in) dollop of tacky glue into the flower centre and sprinkle on some seed beads. Leave to dry.

5. Cut two tissue paper leaves freehand, approximately 8cm (3⅛in) long, and stick to the underside of the flower to hide the wire.

Gather **For each flower:**
- Tissue paper in your chosen colour, or colours if you are going for a variegated
- look: enough for ten 12 x 18cm (4¾ x 7in) rectangles
- Green tissue paper for leaves
- Silver wire (2in length)
- Seed beads for flower centre
- Tacky glue

DAISY BRYAN

Suffolk Puff-ery

The technique of making Suffolk puffs – also called yo-yos – dates back to the Victorian era, when they were made from scraps of fabric sewn together to make patchwork quilts. Use them to great effect on cushion covers and lampshades, using a colour theme to suit the recipient's decor.

1. The fabric circle size needs to be twice the diameter of the finished puff, plus 1.3cm (½in) for a hem. Start by drawing around your circular object onto the back of your fabric with a fabric marker pen, then cut out the circle.

2. Tie a knot in the end of a long piece of strong thread and sew a running stitch along the edge of the circle. To be really neat, fold the edge over as you go to form a basic hem.

3. When you have stitched all the way round the circle hold the fabric and pull the thread through from both ends (find your original knot) to gather it.

4. Pull tight and tie the two ends together, then trim away any excess thread. And there you have a Suffolk puff! Make lots more puffs in the same way.

5. Now you can use your puffs to decorate anything you like – cushions, lampshades, clothes, and so on. For the cushion in the finished photograph, the puffs have been attached with a self-cover fabric button, in a coordinating fabric, added to the centre of each puff.

Gather
- Circular object to draw around to make your Suffolk puff template (see step 1)
- Scraps of fabric
- Fabric marker pen
- Strong thread and needle
- Self-cover fabric buttons

CHARLOTTE ADDISON

Coffee Pot Cosy

This flame-red fabric cosy is the perfect pick you up, even before your first cup of coffee! What a brilliant gift for a special friend!

1. Prepare the cosy template and cut out two of each (a front and a back) from the cosy fabric, the lining fabric and the interlining. Trace the heart template four times onto fusible webbing and roughly cut out the heart shapes. Iron onto the appliqué fabric and cut out neatly. Remove the backing paper from the motifs and position them, glue side down, onto the cosy front and back, placing one above the other centrally.

2. Place the cosy front and back together with right sides facing and pin. Take 5cm (2in) of ribbon, fold in half and place in between the fabric at the centre top, loop facing inwards. Re-pin. Machine stitch with a 6mm (¼in) seam allowance. Turn right side out and press.

3. Place two lining pieces together, right sides facing, and place between the two interlinings.

4. Sew round the edge leaving the bottom open. Put the cosy inside the lining, right sides facing, and align raw edges. Pin, then stitch round the bottom edge leaving a 7.5cm (3in gap). Turn right side out and press.

5. Fold in the edges of the turning gap and pin. Topstitch round the bottom of the cosy about 1.3cm (½in) from the edge. Press.

Gather
- Fabric for cosy outer: one piece measuring 114cm x 50cm (45½in x 20in)
- Fabric for lining and appliqué: one piece measuring 114cm x 50cm (45½in x 20in)
- Medium sew-in interlining
- Fusible webbing
- 5cm (2in) red ribbon
- White sewing thread

Templates for this project can be found at the back of the book. Full-size templates are available at: http://ideas.sewandso.co.uk/patterns

SARAH CALLARD

Quilted Oven Glove

Oven gloves are a really popular make – both for sewers and for the friends who receive them. They bring instant colour to even the drabbest kitchen.

1. Take a piece of paper and draw loosely around the shape of your relaxed hand. Go over the outline, adding an extra 5cm (2in) all around and making sure it comes as far up your wrist as you would like. Cut this out to make your oven glove template.

2. Fold the fabric in half; place the template on the folded fabric and draw around it to give you a front and a back glove. Cut out. Also use the template to cut out front and back pieces from the wadding and a front and back from the lining fabric.

3. Tack (baste) the matching top and lining fabric pieces together with the wadding sandwiched in the middle. Quilt – crisscross lines are simple and effective.

4. With right sides facing, pin the quilted front and back pieces together, adding a loop of ribbon between the layers, making sure that the looped ends are facing inwards. Machine stitch together taking extra care where the thumb meets the rest of the glove.

5. Snip into the seams around the thumb and turn the glove right way out.

6. Cut a 10cm (3⅞in) wide strip of the lining fabric to bind the raw edge of the glove. Fold the fabric strip in half and press. Open up the strip and place one raw edge to the raw edge of the glove and stitch about 1.3cm (½in) from the edge. Fold the strip back over to the inside of the glove, turn under and machine or hem stitch in place.

Gather

For one glove:
- Fabric for glove (see step 1)
- Coordinating fabric for lining and top edge binding
- Insulating wadding (batting)
- Cotton ribbon for hanging loop
- White sewing thread

SUE TREVOR

3D Paper Hearts

A set of pretty 3-dimensional heart decorations, made in three different sizes, will make quite an impact at any celebration.

1. Make card templates of the three different heart shapes required. For each decoration three same-sized paper hearts are used. From a pack of 24 sheets of paper you will be able to make 19 decorations.

2. Use the large heart template to cut large hearts from nine sheets of paper. Cut eight sheets of patterned paper in half and use for cutting out 15 long, thin hearts.

3. Divide the remaining sheets of paper into quarters, and use to cut 30 small hearts.

4. Place the cut out hearts together in matching groups of three. Machine stitch a line down the centre of each group of hearts.

5. Make a hole at the top and bottom of each heart using a large needle. Attach a jump ring through each hole. Tie and double knot a 12cm (4¾in) length of cotton cord to each jump ring.

6. Make a loop for hanging at the top cord. Thread a glass bead onto the bottom cord and tie with a double knot to secure. Your heart decorations are now ready to hang.

Gather
- 24 sheets double-sided patterned paper 30.5cm (12in) square in mixed patterns
- Card for templates
- Pink sewing thread
- 30, 6mm silver jump rings
- Pink cotton cord
- Glass beads

Templates for this project can be found at the back of the book. Full-size templates are available at: http://ideas.sewandso.co.uk/patterns

FIONA PEARCE

Springtime Birdhouse

This wooden birdhouse embellished with springtime papers using the decoupage technique makes a beautiful decoration or table centrepiece.

1. Use a ruler to precisely measure the dimensions of each surface of the birdhouse – you may find it useful to make templates. Cut out a piece of patterned paper for each surface.

2. Apply decoupage glue to the area to be covered, then gently smooth the paper onto the surface with your fingers, pressing firmly to remove any air bubbles. Wipe away excess glue with a damp cloth.

3. Once each surface of the birdhouse is covered with paper, apply another two coats of decoupage glue over all of the paper surfaces, allowing each coat to dry before adding the next.

4. When the paper has completely dried, use a craft knife to cut out the hole on the front of the birdhouse, allowing a small lip of paper to fold over the edge of the hole to give a neat edge. Then cut a thin strip of paper to line the hole, layering it over the lip of paper.

5. Trim the edges of the roof with the ribbon using craft glue to attach it. If you wish, you can add other embellishments too, cutting motifs from patterned papers for example, or using springtime-themed stickers.

Gather

- Birdhouse blank
- Patterned papers; amount required will depend on size of birdhouse (step 1)
- Decoupage and craft glue
- Ruler
- Craft knife
- Ribbon

Please note that the birdhouse is not waterproof and should not be left outside.

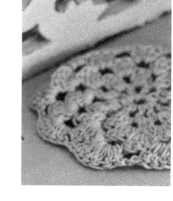

GRACE HARVEY

Crochet Flower Coasters

The perfect project for the newbie crocheter: the pattern is simple to follow, giving you rapid results and a great sense of achievement.

1. Make a coaster following the crochet pattern below:

Foundation ring: Make 7ch, sl st into 1st ch to form ring.

Rnd 1: 2ch (counts as 1st tr), 2ch, *1tr into ring, 2ch, rep from * 8 more times, sl st into 3rd ch at beg of round. (10 spokes coming out of ring)

Rnd 2: Sl st into 1st 2ch sp from previous round, 3ch (counts as 1tr), work 2tr into same ch sp as sl st, 1ch, miss next tr, *3tr into next ch sp, 1ch, rep from * until all ch sp have been worked into, sl st into 3rd ch at beg of round. (10 sections of 3)

Rnd 3: *4tr, then 1ch. Repeat from * 9 times. Sl st through the 1st tr to complete the circle.

Rnd 4: Sl st into 1st 1ch sp from previous round, 4ch (counts as 1tr & 1ch), *miss 4tr, 5tr into next 1ch sp, 1ch, rep from * 8 more times, 4tr into last 1ch space sl st into 3rd of 4ch at beg of round. (10 sections of 4)

Rnd 5: Sl st into 1st 1ch sp from prev round, 4ch (counts as 1tr and 1ch), *miss 5tr, 7tr into next 1ch sp, 1ch, rep from * 8 more times, 6tr into last 1ch space sl st into 3rd of 4ch at beg of round. (10 sections of 7)

2. Break off yarn and sew in loose ends.

3. Pin out on ironing board and cover with damp cloth, press with steam iron.

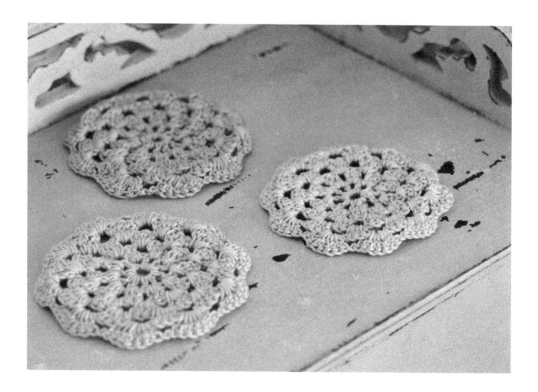

Gather

100% cotton 4-ply:
- 1 x 100g ball turquoise yarn
- 1 x 100g ball lime yarn

- 1 x 100g ball green yarn
- 3mm (US size C/2) crochet hook

- Pins
- Pressing cloth and steam iron

Abbreviations used in pattern

ch chain	sl st slip stitch
ch sp chain space	tr treble (US: double
rep repeat	crochet)

LINDA CLEMENTS

Antique Doily Cushion

This pretty cushion is ideal for using up odd squares of fabric, or displaying some antique lace doilies. If you like to crochet, you could make your own doilies.

1. Make the patchwork by joining six squares together into three rows using 6mm (¼in) seams. Press seams in one direction. Sew a white strip between each row of squares and press. Sew on the top and bottom border strips, then the left-hand strip and press. Don't sew the right border yet.

2. Sew the backing fabric to the bottom of the cushion (along the long edge). Now sew the final border to the right side of the combined patchwork/backing piece. Hem the raw edge of this strip.

3. Sew the doilies to the cushion using matching thread. Add the wadding to the back of the patchwork and machine quilt around the doilies in two circles of zigzag stitch.

4. Fold the patchwork and backing right sides together and sew along the top edge. Turn through and press. Turn the right-hand border in by half its width, press and insert the cushion pad.

5. Position four buttons equally spaced along the right side, with four matching at the back. Sew through each pair of buttons to fasten the cushion.

Gather
- Pastel prints: eighteen 9cm (3½in) squares
- Two strips white print each 4.4 x 47cm (1¾ x 18½in)
- Top/bottom borders: two strips pastel print each 4.4 x 47cm (1¾ x 18½in)
- Left border: one strip pastel print 4.4 x 36.8cm (1¾ x 14½in)
- Right border/lining: one strip pastel print 15.2 x 72.4cm (6in x 28½in)
- Backing fabric: 53.3 x 50.2cm (19¾ x 14½in)
- Wadding (batting) 48.3 x 35.5cm (19 x 14in)
- Two lace doilies
- Eight medium buttons
- Cushion pad

13

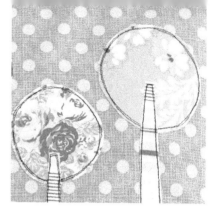

KIRSTY NEALE

Appliqué Trees Cushion

Bright polka dot fabric and lollipop trees appliqué add a touch of spring to a home. It's also a quick and clever way to spruce up some old cushions.

1. To decorate the cushion front with the simple appliqué design, iron fusible webbing onto the reverse side of three contrasting scrap fabrics, draw three circles freehand and cut out. Draw three tree trunk shapes and cut out from fusible-webbing backed striped fabric. Peel off the backing paper, and iron the circles into position, followed by the overlapping trunks, as shown in the finished photograph.

2. Machine a couple of rows of stitches round the edges of the appliqué to hold each piece more securely in place. Don't be too precise, let the rows cross for a relaxed look (see detail photograph).

3. To make the envelope back, first fold over and stitch a narrow double hem down one long edge of each cushion back piece.

4. With right sides facing, pin the hemmed rectangles to the front with hemmed edges overlapping. Machine stitch together round the sides. Remove the pins, then trim the corners to reduce bulk. Turn the cover the right way out through the envelope back. Gently push each corner into shape using a knitting needle. Press the seams flat for a neat finish. Insert a cushion pad (35cm x 35cm/14in x 14in).

Gather
- Fabric for cushion front: one piece 40cm x 40cm (15½in x 15½in)
- Fabric for cushion back: two pieces 40cm x 23cm (15½in x 9in)
- Scraps of fabric for appliqué, including a striped fabric
- Sewing thread
- Fusible webbing
- Knitting needle
- Cushion pad 35 x 35cm (14 x 14in)

MARY FOGG

Striped Tote Bag

Summer's here! Time to pack the cossie and head for the beach. Vibrant fat quarters are used to make this eye-catching tote bag.

1. Choose three different fabrics and from each piece, cut out four 30cm x 8cm (11⅞in x 3½in) strips. You will have 12 strips in total, six for the front of the bag and six for the back. Decide on your preferred layout of strips.

2. Allowing for a 6mm (¼in) seam allowance, pin the first two strips together, right sides facing. Machine stitch along the edge and continue in the same way adding each strip as you go, until the first six strips have been sewn to form the front of your bag. Press seams open on the reverse, then press the front. Repeat for the back.

3. Put the patchwork back and front together with right sides facing. Pin round three sides making sure all seams match up, and leaving the top open. Machine stitch with a 6mm (¼in) seam allowance. Turn inside out and press in a 1.3cm (½in) hem at the top (wrong sides facing).

4. Place the lining pieces together with right sides facing. Pin then machine stitch together just as you did for the main bag following step 3. Put the lining in the main bag; align pressed hems at the top; pin.

5. To make the handles cut 12 9cm x 9cm (3½in x 3½in) pieces (six per handle) and make a patchwork strip (see step 2). Press in half, long sides together and open. Press a 1cm (⅜in) hem along each long side and fold strip over so hems meet; pin, then sew. Place the straps in between the lining and main bag so they are the same distance from each side; pin. Topstitch all the way round the top edge of the bag.

Gather
- Fat quarter fabric pack
- Fabric for bag lining: two pieces 30cm x 35cm (11⅞in x 13⅞in)
- White sewing thread
- Pink ribbon

KIRSTY NEALE

Flower Girl Hoop

This delicate little picture is a combination of stitching and punched paper flowers. It's so lovely you'll probably want to gift it to... yourself.

1. Stretch and secure the linen fabric in your embroidery hoop. Wrap decorative tape around the sides of the hoop, then fold over and press down onto the front edges to decorate.

2. Draw a head and shoulders onto the fabric using a vanishing marker pen. If you're not too confident about your freehand drawing skills

trace the shape from a photograph. Sew over the lines with backstitch, using just two or three strands of grey to keep the lines fine and clear.

3. Punch out tiny flowers from a selection of coloured papers. Arrange them on your original drawing to make a fun flowered hat. Once you're happy with the arrangement,

lift the flowers off one at a time, and fix each to your fabric with a single small cross stitch. Cut a length of red stranded cotton and tie a bow, then stitch it to the girl's collar.

4. Trim away the excess fabric at the back of your hoop. Cut a circle of felt to fit over the back and glue into place for a neat finish.

Gather
- Ivory 32-count linen
- Wooden embroidery hoop
- Decorative tape
- Vanishing marker pen
- Grey and red stranded cotton (floss) plus other colours for
flower 'centre' cross stitch to complement the papers
- Flower punch
- Patterned papers
- White felt
- Tacky glue

FIONA-GRACE PEPPLER

Granny Square Slippers

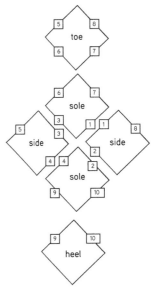

New babies grow so fast you'll be glad to know these gorgeous little slippers are really quick to make!

1. Measure the length of the baby's foot. Divide this measurement in half to give you the diagonal width required for each granny square.

2. Make six crochet squares for each slipper, following the pattern, starting with **MC** yarn and completing the final round in **C** yarn. Two squares laid corner to corner should be as long as baby's foot.

Foundation ring: 4ch, join with sl st to form a ring.

Rnd 1: 1ch, 12dc into ring, join with sl st into 1st ch. (12sts)

Rnd 2: 1ch, 1dc into next dc, *3dc into next dc, 1dc into next 2dc, repeat from * twice, 3dc into next dc, 1dc into last dc, join with sl st into 1st ch. (20sts)

Rnd 3: 1ch, 1dc into next 2dc, *3dc into next dc, 1dc into next 4dc, rep from * twice, 3dc into next dc, 1dc into next 2dc, join with sl st into 1st ch. (28sts)

Rnd 4: 1ch, 1 dc into next 3dc, *3dc into next dc, 1dc into next 6dc, repeat from * twice, 3dc into next dc, 1dc into last 3dc, join with sl st into 1st ch. (28sts)

Keeping pattern correct, work as given until required size is achieved, increasing by working 3dc at each corner, working last round in yarn C.

3. Using a blunt needle and a length of yarn, and following the layout diagram, slip stitch four squares together to form the sole and sides. Slip stitch another square to close up one end by folding the sides in to form the toe. Slip stitch two sides of another square to the opposite end to form the heel.

4. Iron the motifs onto the slippers and reinforce with a few stitches.

5. Securely fasten a button at each side of each corner at the back of the slipper. The buttons can be omitted if you are concerned about safety.

Gather	• 3.5mm (US size E/4) crochet hook	• 1 x 50g ball 3-ply pink **(C)**	**Abbreviations used in pattern**	
	• 1 x 50g ball 3-ply blue yarn **(MC)**	• Dog and cat iron-on motifs	**ch** chain	**sl st** slip stitch
		• Four pink or blue buttons	**dc** double crochet (US: single crochet)	**st/s** stitch/es
			rep repeat	**tr** treble (US: double crochet)

Sweetheart Apron

This retro-style reversible apron has a large heart-shaped pocket on one side. It's perfect for keeping your clothes clean when cooking up a romantic dinner for two.

lengthwise (wrong sides facing); press. Repeat for the two remaining strips to make the waistband/ties.

3. Lay one apron panel right side up; attach frill, raw edges matching, pinning tucks at 2.5cm (1in) intervals; tack (baste) in place. Cut two hearts in fabric B using the template provided; interface one. With hearts right sides together, sew round edge leaving a small gap for turning, then slip stitch closed. Topstitch all round, close to the edge with red thread. Attach the heart to the centre of fabric A, leaving top open to form a pocket.

4. Place the apron panels together right sides facing, so that the frill stays between the panels. Pin and sew; turn right side out.

5. Sew gathering stitches along the top edge. Match middle of waistband to middle of gathered edge. Measure 5cm (2in) beyond the frill edge at either side and mark with a pin. From end of ties sew raw edges up to the pinned marks. Turn the ties right way out and press. Sew waistband to gathered edge of apron (right sides facing). Turn over and slip stitch the other side of the waistband in place. Press to finish.

1. To make a template for the reversible apron panels, cut a piece of paper 67cm x 40cm (26in x 16in) and use a large dinner plate to round off one of the bottom corners of the longest edge. Fold the paper in half and mark the second corner to match. Use this template to cut the reversible apron panels from fabrics A and B.

2. Cut four pieces of fabric B measuring 9cm (3½in) long to the width of the fabric. For a frill, sew two fabric B strips to form one long strip; and press. Fold the frill strip

---

Gather
- Fabric A: 0.5m (20in) 112cm (45in) wide
- Fabric B: 1m (40in) 112cm (45in) wide

- Paper for template
- Red sewing thread
- Fusible interfacing

Templates for this project can be found at the back of the book. Full-size templates are available at: http://ideas.sewandso.co.uk/patterns

ELLEN KHARADE

Cute Egg Cosies

These egg cosies are a perfect gift for the Easter breakfast table. Instructions are given for making the bunny cosy, but you can easily adapt the basic shape to make the alternative designs shown here.

1. Use the bunny back template to cut three pieces of patterned fabric and two pieces of wadding. Use the bunny body template to cut one piece of patterned fabric. Use the bunny face template to cut one piece of white felt. Pin the curved edges of the face to the body, right sides facing; machine stitch. Hand sew ric rac across the middle of the patterned fabric, and flower braid across the fabric change. Sew on the bunny's facial details, using French knots for the eyes, satin and chain stitches for the nose and mouth, and three long stitches for the whiskers.

2. Iron a small piece of fusible webbing to the back of a small piece of the patterned fabric, then use the ear template to cut out two inner ear pieces. Cut two outer ear pieces from white felt. Iron the inner ear pieces in place on the outer ear pieces and machine stitch in place. Tack (baste) the ears to the top of the bunny cosy front, with right sides facing and ears pointing downwards. Pin front and back together, right sides facing.

3. Machine stitch all round leaving the bottom edge open. Sandwich the lining pieces (right sides facing) between the wadding pieces. Pin, then machine sew to leave bottom edge open. Turn lining through to the right side, push into the cosy shell (right sides facing) and pin. Machine sew along one side

of the bottom edge. Turn the right way out, push the lining into the cosy, and sew along the other side. Hand sew ribbon round the bottom edge.

Templates for this project can be found at the back of the book. Full-size templates are available at: http://ideas.sewandso. co.uk/patterns

Alternative design: Using the template provided, follow the cutting instructions for the plain cosy given with the template. Stitch the top and bottom sections together for the front and back, then stitch flower braid across the fabric change. With the finished photograph as a guide, add ric rac, ribbon and any additional embellishments you wish to use, such as seed beads or buttons. To make the flower shown, cut five petals in felt using the template provided. Pinch the narrow ends together, making a fold in the petal. Gather and sew the ends together, attach a button as a flower centre, then stitch the flower to the cosy.

Gather

- Small pieces of patterned fabric and white felt
- Lightweight wadding (batting)
- Ric rac and matching sewing thread to attach
- Narrow flower braid
- Cotton ribbon
- Scrap of fusible webbing
- Brown and pink stranded cotton (floss) for the facial
- details; co-ordinating cotton (floss) to hand stitch ribbon
- White sewing thread

MARION ELLIOT

Cottage Tea Cosy

Here's the perfect gift for a friend who's moving house. The first thing out of the packing case is the teapot, which, of course, must have a tea cosy.

the motifs using a medium stitch and black thread. Outline the windows, lintels and transom, and add crosses to represent panes of glass. Sew lines down the door for panels.

4. Pin the cosy front and the cosy back to the wadding; cut out and machine stitch using a 1cm (⅜in) seam allowance. Pin front and back together, right sides facing. Insert and pin a loop of ribbon between the top seams, facing inwards. Machine stitch together, using a 1cm (⅜in) seam allowance. Trim the seams and turn through.

5. Pin the lining front and back together and machine stitch round the sides using a 1cm (⅜in) seam allowance. Leave the lining wrong side out, and pull it over the cosy, then pin, matching side seams and lower raw edges.

6. Machine stitch round the lower edge of the cosy, leaving a 10cm (3⅞in) gap at the back. Turn through to the right side and slip stitch the gap closed. Sew a button to the door for a handle and to the base of the ribbon loop.

1. Trace and transfer the tea cosy templates to your chosen fabrics and cut out the front, back and linings.

2. Trace and transfer the roof, windows and doors to fusible webbing; cut out roughly. Iron onto your chosen fabrics and cut

out neatly. Remove the backing paper and position the motifs onto the cosy front. Iron in place.

3. Stitch straight lines across the roof in light brown thread to represent tiles. Using freehand machine embroidery, stitch round

Gather
- Fabric for tea cosy front, back and lining: two pieces 35cm x 30cm (13⅞in x 11⅞in); two pieces 35cm x 25cm (13⅞in x 9⅞in)
- Scraps of fabric for appliqué
- Fusible webbing
- Wadding (batting)
- Black, light brown and cream sewing threads
- Ribbon
- Buttons for door handle and ribbon loop

Templates for this project can be found at the back of the book. Full-size templates are available at: http://ideas.sewandso.co.uk/patterns

ALI BURDON

Stitched Lavender Bag

This sweet little project, decorated with a simple satin and cross stitch design, would make a thoughtful gift for someone feeling a bit under the weather.

1. Iron the interlining onto the wrong sides of the fabric pieces following the manufacturer's instructions.

2. Using a dressmaker's pencil or pen, mark a grid in the centre of the right side of one of the pieces of fabric, making the lines around 6mm (¼in) apart.

3. Set your sewing machine to make a satin stitch 2mm in length and 0.5mm in width; stitch along the inner lines of your grid, or make the satin stitch by hand.

4. Work across the grid from left to right, and without cutting the thread between the lines, turn the fabric through 90 degrees and work across the grid from left to right the other way. Finally sew round the outer edge of the grid (this will hide all the uncut threads) and fasten off.

5. Use different coloured stranded cotton to sew cross stitches in the grid squares, using three strands in the needle. It is not necessary to cut the thread between stitches, but don't pull it too tight or you will pucker the fabric.

6. Fasten off each colour set of stitches by taking your needle and thread through the back of a couple of grid stitches.

7. Fold the ric rac in half and pin to the corner of the decorated fabric square, loop pointing down. Place the other fabric square on top, right sides facing; machine stitch together with a 1cm (⅜in) seam allowance leaving a 4cm (1½in) turning gap. Trim seam to 6mm (¼in) and trim corners. Turn right side out, press, and stuff with lavender. Sew the gap closed with an invisible ladder stitch.

Gather

- White cotton fabric for bag: two pieces 11cm x 11cm (4⅜in x 4⅜in)
- Stranded cotton (floss) in a variety of colours
- Medium fusible interlining: two pieces 11cm x 11cm (4⅜in x 4⅜in)
- 24cm (9½in) red ric rac
- Dried lavender
- Dressmaker's pencil or pen

Macramé Bracelet

This elegant macramé bracelet, made using half hitch knots and large glass beads for decoration, would make a stylish 18th birthday gift.

1. Cut two lengths of cotton cord each measuring 30cm (12in), and one length measuring 150cm (60in). Take the two short lengths and tape at each end onto the work surface positioning them side by side. These are your 'core' cords.

2. Tie the longer length of cord around the two core cords using an overhand knot and taking care to make sure that the tails are the same length. Pass the left tail under the core cords and pull through leaving a largish loop on the left

side of the core cords. Pass that tail over the tail on the right side.

3. Lift the right tail over the core cords and down through the loop on the left side. Pull the cords through to make a half hitch knot. Work several more knots to make a 1cm (⅜in) block of macramé.

4. Thread a silver bead onto the core threads. Take the tails either side of the bead and work another 2cm (¾in) block of macramé. Repeat twice.

5. Slide the large-hole glass bead onto the twisted cord. *Add a silver bead and work another 2cm (¾in) macramé block. Repeat from *.

6. Work 1cm (⅜in) of macramé to finish. Trim tails to 2cm (¾in). Remove the tape and form the bracelet into a round shape with the tails facing in opposite directions.

7. Tie a 30cm (12in) length of cord around the four core cords. Work a 2cm (¾in) length of macramé. Add drops of strong glue to secure the tails making sure the slider still slides. Tie the core threads together at each end. Trim tails once dry.

Gather
- Blue cotton cord: three lengths 30cm (12in); one length 150cm (60in)
- Six 6mm antique silver round metallic beads
- Large-hole light blue glass bead
- Tape
- Strong glue

JENNIFER GRACE

Family Photo Hoop

Make a great keepsake for Mother's Day or Father's Day by decorating an embroidery hoop with a family photo, framed with patterned paper flowers.

1. Put a drop of hot glue at the top back of the outer circle of the hoop, and attach the end of the gold thread. Spiral the thread tightly around the hoop to cover it neatly, adding another drop of glue to secure it when you get back to the start. Place the linen fabric into the hoop, stretching it out and tightening the hoop.

2. Trim your photograph to 13cm x 10cm (5in x 4in). Use double-sided tape to attach your photograph to a piece of patterned paper measuring 15cm x 13cm (6in x 5in), then attach this in turn to a piece of contrasting patterned paper measuring 15cm (6in) square. Use hot glue to adhere the layered panel so that it is slightly off centre on the hoop.

3. Punch some flowers from the other three sheets of paper and attach to opposite corners of the photo panel, using hot glue. Add a scattering of small buttons, again using hot glue. If you are using brads, pierce some holes to fit them through the fabric. Trim away any excess material at the back of your hoop. You could neaten the back by adding a circle of white felt.

Gather
- Embroidery hoop 20cm (10in) diameter
- Gold metallic crochet thread
- White linen fabric
- Photograph
- Patterned papers: five to match the colours in the photograph
- Small flower punches
- Buttons and (optional) brads
- Hot glue gun
- Double-sided tape

KIRSTY NEALE

Retro Mobile Case

The classic red telephone box, a very British icon, makes a quirky cover for your mobile phone that's super fast to make!

1. Copy the phone box template onto felt and cut out twice. Draw an 8.5 x 6.5cm (3¼ x 2½in) rectangle onto fusible web, iron onto the back of your patterned fabric and cut out. Peel away the backing paper and iron the rectangle onto one of the felt phone box pieces.

2. Machine stitch round the edges of the patterned rectangle, using black thread. Add two extra vertical lines of stitching and two horizontally to create a window pane effect. Stitch over all lines a second time to create an optional sketchy look.

3. Print the word 'TELEPHONE' onto an inkjet-friendly fabric sheet, using a simple, elegant font. It should measure roughly 6 x 1cm (2⅜ x ⅜in). Cut out, leaving a narrow border around the word. Stitch into place on the felt phone box, just above the patterned fabric rectangle.

4. Again using black thread, stitch twice round the top part of the felt phone box, as marked on the template. Cut a 3.5cm (1⅜in) piece of ribbon and fold it in half. Pin to one side of the felt phone box piece, just below the stitched section.

5. Pin the decorated felt piece to the plain one, so the ribbon ends are sandwiched in between. Sew along the sides and bottom edge to join the two pieces together, using a double line of stitches, as before.

Gather
- Red felt
- Fusible web
- Patterned fabric
- Black thread
- Inkjet-friendly fabric
- Computer and printer
- 3.5cm (1⅜in) piece cotton ribbon

Templates for this project can be found at the back of the book. Full-size templates are available at: http://ideas.sewandso.co.uk/patterns

KIRSTY NEALE

Vintage Paper Bracelet

Cylindrical beads made from vintage papers, old book pages, maps, gift wrap and such like, can be strung into a pretty, personalized bracelet.

1. Copy the bead template onto paper and cut it out. Spread a thin layer of PVA glue over the reverse side, as shown on the template. Starting at the narrow end, roll the paper around a cocktail stick. Press the sticky wider end down firmly to secure.

2. Slide the paper bead off the cocktail stick and leave to dry. Make 25–30 beads in this way. When they're all dry, brush on one or two coats of varnish to seal and protect the paper.

3. Fold the length of jewellery wire in half, then twist a little way below the fold to create a small loop. Slide a round bead onto one of the wire ends, followed by a paper bead, and then another round bead.

4. Feed the other wire end through the three beads in the opposite direction. Pull both wires taut so the paper bead sits flat and centred below the twisted wire loop. Add more beads in the same way.

5. When your bracelet reaches the desired length, twist the remaining wire ends together and snip off any excess. Carefully bend the twisted wire into a hook-shaped closure. Slip this through the loop at the opposite end to wear your finished bracelet.

Gather
- Vintage papers
- PVA glue
- Cocktail stick (or toothpick)
- Clear varnish
- 3m (3½yd) jewellery wire
- Small round crystal beads
- Pliers (optional)

Templates for this project can be found at the back of the book.
Full-size templates are available at:
http://ideas.sewandso.co.uk/patterns

LISA FORDHAM

Posh Peg Bag

This clothes peg bag is made of hard-wearing laminated cloth to keep it smart for ages. It's a great way to brighten up your laundry day.

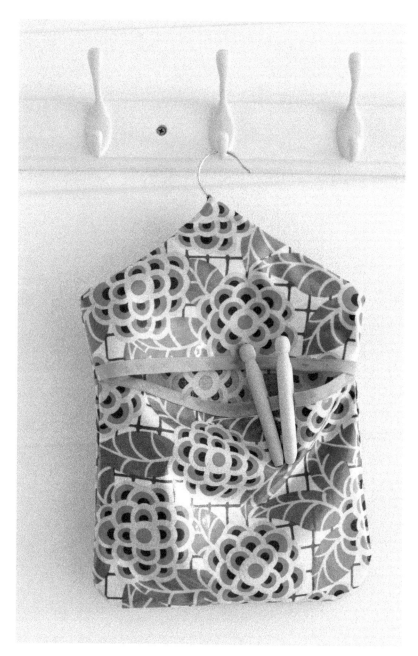

1. Using the template draw one back and two front pieces on the laminated fabric, allowing an extra 1cm (⅜in) seam allowance all around. Line up the coat hanger and bend to fit the top of the bag. Set the hanger aside.

2. Carefully cut out one back piece of laminated fabric and two front pieces ensuring that you have enough fabric to overlap at the opening. Lay out your two front pieces right side up and cut two lengths of bias binding to fit along the top of the bottom piece, and the bottom of the top piece (the bag opening). With right sides together, fold the binding lengthways over the top of the bottom front and pin into position. Repeat on the bottom of the top piece. Machine stitch into place using a 1cm (⅜in) seam allowance.

3. With right sides together, pin the back, bottom front and top front together, with a 1cm (⅜in) overlap at the opening. The binding on the bottom front should sit neatly behind the binding at the top.

4. Mark the area where the coat hanger comes through the top of the bag using a pin each side of the 3cm (1¼in) space for the hanger. Pin, tack and then starting at the top of the bag carefully machine stitch all round using a 1cm (⅜in) seam. Turn the bag right side out and slip in the hanger. Wrap plastic tape around the hook to finish, if required.

Gather
- Laminated fabric 0.25m (¼yd) x 54–56cm (21¼–22in) wide
- Bias binding 60cm (24in) x 2.5cm (1in) wide, cut in two equal pieces
- Wire coat hanger
- Plastic tape (optional)

Templates for this project can be found at the back of the book. Full-size templates are available at: http://ideas.sewandso.co.uk/patterns

CLAIRE GARLAND

Cute Vintage Purse

This pretty little knitted purse with its cross stitch bloom is a charming gift for a little girl. Just don't forget to pop a lucky coin inside first.

1. Front then back of purse

Tension (US: gauge): *21sts x 28 rows = 10cm (4in) in stocking stitch.*

Cast on 22sts. Beg with a k row, work 15 rows st st. Place marker at each end of next row to mark 'Hinge Point'.

Row 16: Kf&b, p20, kf&b. 24sts
St st 2 rows.

Row 19: K1, m1 to the right, k to last st, m1 to the left, k1. 26sts

Row 20: Kf&b, p to last st, kf&b. 28sts

Row 21: K14, place marker on last stitch to mark beg of motif (red dot on chart). St st 9 rows.

Row 31: K2 tog, k to last 2 sts, k2 tog.

Row 32: P1, p2 tog, p to last 3sts, p2 tog, p1. 24sts

St st 2 rows.
Place marker at each end of next row to mark 'Hinge Point'.

Row 35: Skpo, k20, k2 tog. 22sts.
St st 15 rows. Cast off (bind off). Press.

2. Cross stitch the motif, beginning at red dot on chart.

3. Using purse frame and knitted panel, make a template to cut the lining, marking hinge markers and allowing 1cm (⅜in) seam around sides and top edges. Cut lining piece. Fold knitted panel in half, right sides together. Backstitch side seams from hinge point down both sides. Turn out. Fold the fabric panel in half, with right sides together. Sew side seams

from the hinge point down both sides. Press the seam allowance from hinge and top edge on fabric panel to wrong sides. Tack lining the inside the purse, wrong sides together.

4. Apply glue to one side of the frame and to top and side edges of fabric around one side of opening. Insert one side of purse into frame, starting at the hinge. Check lining is even. Allow to dry. Repeat on the other side.

Abbreviations used in knitting pattern	
k knit	**p** purl
kf&b knit into front & back of st (1 st made)	**skpo** slip 1 st, knit 1 st, pass slipped st over (1 st decreased)
k/p2 tog knit/purl 2 together (1 st decreased)	**st st** stocking st (US: stockinette st) (alternate k&p rows)
m1 make 1 st	**st/s** stitch/es

KEY

■ deep red	■ bright pink	□ pea green
■ dark orange	■ light pink	□ light aqua
■ bright orange	■ dark green	• dot should match marker

Stitch count: 18H x 20W
Each coloured square represents a cross stitch worked over a knitted stitch

Gather
- Half a 50g (1¾oz) ball of cream DK yarn
- Lengths 4-ply or crewel wool (used double) to match charted motif
- Vintage fabric 46 x 55cm (18 x 22in) for lining
- 4.5mm (US size 7) knitting needles
- Tapestry needle
- Purse frame 10 x 5cm (4 x 2in)
- Suitable clear drying glue

DANIELLE LOWY

Suffolk Puff Rings

Suffolk puffs are ideal for showing off vintage buttons. We've turned ours into flamboyant rings, but you could add a brooch back or small hair clip instead, or make three puffs and sew them to ribbon for a necklace.

1. Using a mug or bowl, trace an 8cm (3¼in) diameter circle on the fabric and cut it out.

2. Double thread your needle and knot the end. With the knot on the right side of the material, sew small running stitches round the circle about 5mm (¼in) in from the edge. Leave the needle threaded.

3. Pull the thread from the needle end to create a showercap-like shape. Flatten it and sew a few stitches across the centre to secure it.

4. Keeping the same needle and thread, sew the button onto the pleated side. You can sew right through to the other side of the material to make it secure. Knot and cut the thread.

5. Using a glue gun or strong all-purpose glue, attach the ring base to the back of the Suffolk puff. Stand back and admire!

Gather
- Cotton fabric 10 x 10cm (4 x 4in)
- Mug or bowl, 8cm (3¼in) diameter
- Fancy or vintage button
- Ring base
- Matching thread
- Glue gun or strong all-purpose glue

KIRSTY NEALE

Jelly Mould Candles

Small, vintage jelly moulds made of metal or glass, are filled with a wick and melted wax to make these simple but striking candles. They're quick, inexpensive, but always welcome gifts.

1. Cut a length of wick, 5cm (2in) taller than the height of the mould. Thread one end through a metal wick-holder and place in the bottom of the mould. Tie the other end around a pencil. Rest this across the top of the mould to hold the wick in position.

2. Place your wax in a heatproof bowl and place the bowl over a saucepan half-filled with water. Gently heat the water until the wax in the bowl is completely melted. Stir in a few drops of essential oil if you want to make a scented candle.

3. Carefully pour the liquid wax into the mould, and allow to cool for 30–60 minutes.

4. As the wax hardens, a well or dip is likely to form in the centre. To even out the surface, melt a small amount of wax and use a cocktail stick to make holes around the wick. Pour the melted wax carefully on top.

5. Trim the wick so only 1cm (⅜in) or so is visible above the top of the wax. Set your finished candle aside for 24 hours before lighting.

Gather
- Small vintage jelly mould
- Candle wick
- Metal wick-holder
- Candle wax
- Saucepan
- Heatproof bowl to fit inside saucepan
- Essential oil (optional)
- Pencil
- Cocktail stick

DANIELLE LOWY

Paper Bead Bracelets

As an alternative to chocolate or sweets, give these handmade bracelets as a unique gift. The cute egg-shaped beads and pretty pastel colours are sure to delight all ages!

1. Each bead is made from a long triangle of paper. First mark out the triangles onto the back of your paper sheets: make a pencil mark every 2cm (¾in) down the right-hand side; on the left-hand side, make the first mark at 1cm (⅜in), then all subsequent marks 2cm (¾in) apart.

2. To join the pencil marks, draw a line from the top right-hand corner to the 1cm (⅜in) mark on the left-hand side, then draw a line from the 1cm (⅜in) mark to the first 2cm (¾in) mark on the right-hand side, and carry on zigzagging down to the bottom of the sheet.

3. Cut out the triangles, discarding those marked first and last on the paper sheet.

4. Take a paper triangle and starting at the wide end, roll it snugly round a cocktail stick. Glue the last 10cm (4in) to keep the paper from unfurling, then place the cocktail stick in a foam block. Make nine more beads in the same way.

5. Apply a coat of sealing varnish to the beads and leave to dry; then apply another coat of varnish to ensure strong shiny beads. When completely dry, twist the beads off the cocktail sticks.

6. Cut a 30cm (12in) length of elastic cord and attach a paper clip about 5cm (2in) from one end. Thread on paper beads interspersed with seed beads – the number required will depend on the wrist size. Remove the paper clip and tie the ends together tightly in a knot. Cut off excess cord.

Gather
- Sheets of patterned paper 15cm x 15cm (6in x 6in)
- Seed beads
- 30cm (12in) elastic cord
- Sealing varnish
- Foam block
- Cocktail sticks

FIONA-GRACE PEPPLER

Vintage Sewer's Helper

A pretty teacup and some old-fashioned tricks can keep pins and needles clean and sharp, ready for any sewing project. Your sewing-mad relation will be intrigued by this clever gift.

1. Glue the magnets to the inside of the teacup, low down, but not on the base. These will capture pins, needles and scissors placed in the saucer for safekeeping. Glue the teacup into the saucer and set aside to dry.

2. Make the pincushion by cutting a circle of cotton about three times larger than the top of the cup. Hand sew a ring of running stitch about 5mm (¼in) in from the raw edge, but don't fasten off.

3. Pull on your sewing thread to gather the circle. Stuff the ball with bird grit. This will keep your pins rust free and sharpen them when you use it. Close the puff and fasten off tightly.

4. Create a smaller cushion in the same way to fit the bowl of your teaspoon, but this time stuff it with fine wire wool. This is your needle sharpener – but don't store your needles here, as they will rust. Carefully glue the pad into the spoon.

5. Now assemble the final pieces by positioning the pincushion into the cup and carefully gluing into place.

Gather	• Vintage teacup and saucer	• Strong magnets	• Superglue or
	• Vintage teaspoon	• Bird grit (from pet shops)	ceramic cement
	• Coordinating cotton (step 2)	• Fine wire wool	

ELSIE MOLYNEUX of Elsie Mo Flowers

Tin Flower Centrepiece

This easy project is a great way to recycle old tins, jars and crockery to bring the outdoors in. Use any variety of fresh flowers that are in season.

1. Cut your floral foam to the right size for your chosen container and soak it by floating it in a bowl full of water. It will absorb and sink when it's ready (don't force it under). Fill your container to the lip with floral foam so it reaches all the edges.

2. Choose a natural looking selection of flowers from your garden or florist shop (so you can buy stems individually). Don't over complicate the look of the design, try to stick to no more than four or five different flower types as different from each other as possible. Smaller flower heads are easier to work with, and picking a colour scheme also helps.

3. Insert your flowers and foliage into the floral foam in an upright manner to resemble natural growing formations. Disperse them randomly to cover the whole surface of the foam. Add grasses and a touch of foliage to add to the garden theme.

4. Finally, fill in the gaps evenly between the flowers with moss to create a lawn like effect. Moss can be bought in garden centres or you may be lucky enough to find it in your garden. Alternatively, small stones, pebbles or decorative gravel could be used.

Gather
- One block of floral foam
- Vintage container
- Moss or small stones/pebbles
- Variety of fresh flowers
- Grasses or foliage (e.g. bear grass)

ELLEN KHARADE

Retro Curtain Bag

A bag made from vintage curtain material, teamed up with corduroy fabric and large chunky buttons – perfect for carrying all those essential bits and bobs.

1. Pin the template for the bag to the curtain material and cut one shape for the front and one for the back. With a bold pattern such as the one used here, you will need to spend a little time working out how to place the template so that the pattern falls as you wish.

2. Decide which piece will be the back. Cut an 35 x 8cm (13¾ x 3⅛in) strip from the corduroy, pin and machine stitch to the top of the vintage fabric. Cut a strip of ric rac and stitch across the fabric change.

3. Make the front of the bag in the same way but then decorate the floral motifs with beads and sequins and sew three large chunky buttons across the corduroy fabric.

4. Cut a 3 x 12cm (1¼ x 4¾in) strip of floral fabric and fold in half. Machine stitch up the side with a 6mm (¼in) seam allowance and thread through the wooden handle, then stitch to the top of the bag. Attach the other three handle tabs in the same way.

5. With right sides facing, pin the front and back together and stitch with a 1cm (⅜in) seam allowance. Cut the lining fabric the same size as the bag shell using the template. With right sides facing pin the lining together and machine stitch.

6. Turn the bag the right way and press carefully, avoiding the beads and sequins. Turn the lining the wrong way and press down a 1.3cm (½in) hem at the raw edge. Push the lining into the bag and stitch into place using neat slip stitches round the top edge of the bag.

Gather
- Vintage curtain fabric: two pieces 40 x 30cm (15¾ x 12in)
- Blue corduroy fabric 0.25m (¼yd)

- Coordinating lining fabric: two pieces 40 x 38 cm (15¾ x 15in)
- Blue ric rac 1m (1yd)
- Three large chunky buttons

- Selection of beads and sequins
- Two wooden bag handles
- Coordinating threads

Templates for this project can be found at the back of the book. Full-size templates are available at: http://ideas.sewandso.co.uk/patterns

JENNY ARNOTT

Hanging Fabric Hearts

These sweet fabric hearts, filled with dried lavender, would make lovely fragrant wedding favours or gifts for the bridal party.

1. For each heart, cut two fabric heart shapes from floral fabric using the template provided.

2. Cut a length of ribbon 13cm (5in) long and fold in half. (You might want to make a number of hearts and hang them at different drops. If so, vary the lengths of ribbon you cut at this stage.) Sandwich the ribbon with loop facing down between the front and back heart pieces (right sides together) at the top edge. Machine stitch all round the heart with a 6mm (¼in) seam allowance, leaving a 4cm (1½in) gap open along one side. Clip the curves, then turn the heart right side out.

3. Press well before filling the the heart with dried lavender. Close the opening with neat hand stitches and matching thread. Add a decorative button at the base of the ribbon to finish.

Gather
- Floral patterned fabrics
- Patterned ribbons: for a special celebration, message ribbons are available
- Buttons
- Dried lavender

Templates for this project can be found at the back of the book. Full-size templates are available at: http://ideas.sewandso.co.uk/patterns

KIRSTY NEALE

Vintage Doily Coasters

These tea-party coasters are made by pressing a vintage doily onto circles of white modelling clay for added texture and decoration.

1. Break off a piece of clay and soften it by rolling between your palms. Place on a flat surface and roll out to a thickness of about 1cm (⅜in).

2. Place a vintage doily on top, so that the edge covers around half of the clay. Press it down gently, first with your fingers and then with a rolling pin. Carefully peel the doily off and set it aside.

3. Using a large cookie cutter or the rim of a round metal container, cut out a circle from the clay. Position your cutter so you include some plain clay and some with the doily impression. Leave the clay to dry, according to the instructions on the packaging.

4. To seal the clay, as well as give it a glossy, porcelain-like finish, brush or spray on two or three coats of clear varnish. Make sure you allow each layer to dry before adding the next.

5. Finally, cut out a piece of felt the same size as the finished coaster. Glue it to the base of the clay, to protect your table from scratches and add a subtle splash of colour to your tea party table.

Gather
- White air-drying clay
- Rolling pin
- Vintage doily
- Large cookie cutter or round metal container
- Clear varnish
- Thick coloured felt in a combination of intense colours

LINDA CLEMENTS

Patchwork Coasters

Here's a simple project for someone who's new to patchwork: pretty fabrics arranged in a nine-square block, quilted with a folksy flower and leaf pattern.

1. Take the four polka dot squares, the four print squares and the white square and arrange as shown in the photograph. Using 6mm (¼in) seams, sew the nine squares together. Press the seams.

2. Copy the quilting pattern and tape it to a window. Tape the patchwork on top, right side up, so the pattern shows through in the middle of the patchwork. Use a pencil to *lightly* trace the quilting pattern onto the fabric.

3. Take the 15.2cm (6in) square of wadding and safety pin on the back of the patchwork. Quilt using three strands of stranded cotton. Start with a dark pink French knot in the flower centre, then quilt the traced pattern, stitching through

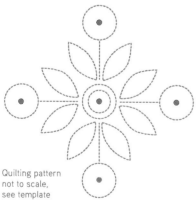

Quilting pattern
not to scale,
see template

both layers, working the flowers in dark pink and leaves in green.

4. Place the patchwork right side *up*. Put the square of backing fabric right side *down* on top of the patchwork and pin together.

5. Trim the wadding and backing to the same size as the patchwork. Machine stitch together all the way

round the edge leaving a gap of about 5.cm (2in) in one side. Trim the corners a little, turn through to the right side and press.

6. Turn the edges of the gap inwards neatly and hand sew together with little stitches and matching thread. Machine sew all round the edge of the mat for a neat, firm edge.

Gather

- Fabric for coaster top: nine pieces measuring 5.7cm x 5.7cm (2¼in x 2¼in)
- Fabric for coaster back: one piece measuring 15.2cm x 15.2cm (6in x 6in)
- Wadding (batting)
- Dark pink and green stranded cotton (floss)

Templates for this project can be found at the back of the book. Full-size templates are available at: http://ideas.sewandso.co.uk/patterns

LINDA CLEMENTS

Ribbon Memory Board

This notice board is perfect to display photos and mementoes of baby's first year. The size of the board can be increased by using larger squares.

1. Cut sixteen 10.2cm (4in) squares from plain fabric and nine from print fabric. Arrange alternately, with one square in the first row, three in the second row, then five, seven, five, three and one.

2. Sew the squares in each row together using 6mm (¼in) seams and press. Sew the rows to each other and press. Trim off the triangles to make the patchwork square but don't cut up to the points – leave 6mm (¼in).

3. Cut two fabric strips 5cm x 38cm (2in x 15in) and two 5cm x 46cm (2in x 18in). Sew the shorter strips to the sides and longer strips to top and bottom. Press seams.

4. Pin the wadding on the back and quilt using the piglet template. Copy the template on to thin card and cut out. Trace round the shapes on to the fabric with a pencil and then quilt with three strands of dark orange stranded cotton. Work the mouth in backstitch and the eye as French knot. Cut strips of ribbon to go across the diagonal lines of the patchwork and overlap to the back. Pin in place, keeping the ribbon taut, and sew through at the intersections. Press and sew buttons at the intersections.

5. Put the patchwork on the corkboard and use a hot glue gun to glue in place at the back, keeping the work straight. Glue ric rac round the edge. Glue a ribbon hanging loop at the back and a sheet of card over the back to finish neatly.

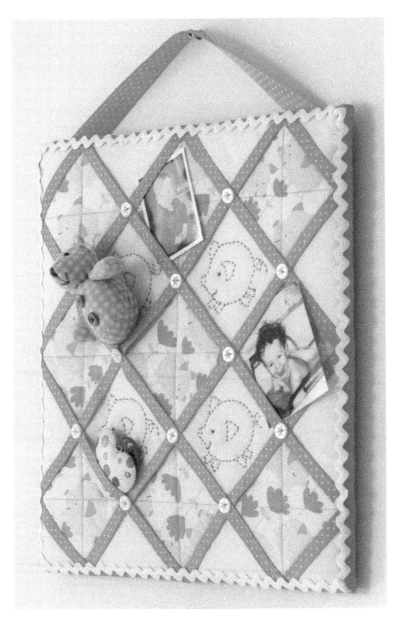

Templates for this project can be found at the back of the book. Full-size templates are available at: http://ideas.sewandso.co.uk/patterns

Gather
- Fat quarter print fabric and 0.5m (½yd) plain fabric
- Wadding (batting) 38cm (15in) square
- Corkboard 38cm (15in) square
- 6m (6½yd) of 1.3cm (½in) wide and 0.5m
- (½yd) 1in wide orange polka dot ribbon
- Dark orange stranded cotton (floss)
- 2m (2yd) white ric rac
- 12 buttons
- Card 38cm (15in) square
- Hot glue gun

37

VERITY GRAVES-MORRIS

Beaded Braid Bracelet

What better way could there be to show how much you care about someone than to make them a friendship bracelet? These are beaded for greater effect.

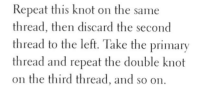

1. Pick threads in three colours. Take the first colour thread and cut it so that the length is the distance from your fingertip to your shoulder. Repeat this until you have six pieces of stranded cotton in total – two pieces per colour. Then tie one big knot with all the threads.

2. To hold the bracelet in place while you're making it, put a safety pin through the knotted end and pin it to a cushion.

3. Take the far left thread and make a forward knot. The first thread on the left is always the primary.

Repeat this knot on the same thread, then discard the second thread to the left. Take the primary thread and repeat the double knot on the third thread, and so on.

4. Start the next row using the thread to the far left. This now becomes your primary thread. Repeat all the steps until you have the row done.

5. Once you've produced some rows, thread a needle through the first thread. Thread the needle through a seed bead, and pull it up tight to the rows. You could thread the stranded cotton directly through the seed bead if it is easier. Put up to four beads on the thread, then secure with a single knot. Repeat this with each piece of thread.

6. Continue knotting the thread (as in step 3), breaking it up intermittently with a few rows of beads. Keep going until the bracelet is long enough to fit around your wrist comfortably To make that sure it fits well, try it on your wrist – there should be enough for you to fit two fingers in next to your wrist, since the bracelet can shrink in water and become too tight (although it will stretch back out when dry).

Gather
- Pastel seed bead pack
- Shades of DMC stranded cotton (floss): 3 per bracelet
- Safety pins

MARION ELLIOT

Bird mp3-Player Case

Your friend will be all a-twitter when you gift her this chirpy little birdy. The appliqué motif is a great excuse to get creative with your scrap fabric stash.

1. Trace all the pieces of the bird and branch template onto fusible webbing and cut out roughly. Iron them onto your chosen appliqué fabrics and cut out neatly.

2. Remove the backing paper from the motifs and position them, onto the top half of the main fabric. Iron into place. Machine stitch round the motifs using a medium stitch and contrasting thread to appliqué them to the fabric.

3. Iron on a lightweight wadding to the back of the main fabric, and fold the main fabric in half with right sides facing. Insert and pin a loop of ribbon between the side seams, facing inwards.

4. Using a 1cm (⅜in) seam allowance, machine stitch round the sides and bottom edge to within 3cm (1⅛in) of the top edge, to make the case. Repeat for the lining fabric. Turn the case through to the right side but not the lining.

5. Insert the case into the lining. Pin and machine stitch the top edge of the case and lining together, right sides facing. Leave a 1.5cm (⅝in) gap above the top of the side seam at either side. Turn lining through to inside.

6. Machine stitch a 1.5cm (⅝in) wide channel across the front and back of the case and thread ribbon through it. Thread on the bead and knot the ribbon ends. Attach a clip to the ribbon loop.

Gather

- Fabric for case and lining: Two pieces 40cm x 10cm (15½in x 3⅞in)
- Scraps of fabric for appliqué
- White and black sewing thread
- Fusible webbing and wadding (batting)
- Ribbon, bead and clip ring

Templates for this project can be found at the back of the book.
Full-size templates are available at:
http://ideas.sewandso.co.uk/patterns

SAMANTHA HORN

Button Box Necklace

Vintage buttons are often a neglected part of fashion so why not make this stylish necklace with an attractive selection of them?

1. Lay your chosen buttons out on a piece of felt. A slightly curved shape is best to create a bib-style necklace around 10–15cm (4–6in) long. When you are happy with your design, use a good quality fabric glue to fix them in place. Leave for five to ten minutes to dry.

2. Use a needle and thread and sew each of the buttons to the felt with a couple of stitches. Carefully cut around your buttons remembering to leave a little either side of the design for the eyelets.

3. Punch a small hole in the felt either side of the design where you will attach the chain. Place the eyelet through the hole and use the eyelet tool to hammer down on the eyelet securing it. (Follow the instructions for the particular eyelet tool you are using.)

4. Using some wire cutters, cut your chain in half. Use pliers to open the jump ring and hook it through the eyelet and the last link in one half on the chain. Use the pliers again to carefully close it so the chain is nicely secured to the felt.

5. Secure the other half of your chain with another jump ring in the same way as before. Your necklace is now ready to wear!

Gather
- Vintage buttons in a variety of sizes; sew-through and flat-shank buttons work best
- Felt sheet
- Fabric glue
- Two 5mm (¼in) eyelets
- Eyelet tool
- Chain 40cm (16in)
- Two 5mm (¼in) jump rings
- Wire cutters
- Pliers
- Needle and thread

MARION ELLIOT

Bow Make-up Purse

This purse would make a perfect first make-up bag for a young granddaughter who is just discovering the delights of the cosmetics counter!

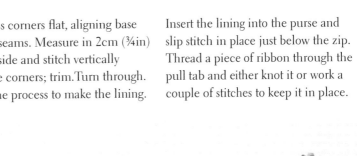

1. Using the pattern, cut a purse front and back and two linings. Iron the interlining to the reverse of the front and back.

2. Take the fabric strips for the bow, and press under and machine hem the long sides. Machine one end of each tie to the sides of the purse front. Hem the free ends. Stitch along the middle of each tie for 11cm (4⅜in) from the side of the purse front. Tie the ends in a bow.

3. Pin the top of the purse front, face down, to the upper edge of the zip, lining up the raw edge with the top of the zip. Tack (baste) in place. Pin the top of the purse back to the lower edge of the zip as before and tack (baste).

4. Machine stitch the zip in place; remove the tacking (basting). Place the purse right side up. Attach the zipper foot. Open the zip halfway, then stitch along both sides of the zip, close to the turned edge.

5. Pin the purse front and back together, with right sides facing, pinning a ribbon loop between the side seams, pointing in. Machine stitch leaving the top edge open. Press open seams.

6. Press corners flat, aligning base and side seams. Measure in 2cm (¾in) at either side and stitch vertically across the corners; trim. Turn through. Repeat the process to make the lining.

Insert the lining into the purse and slip stitch in place just below the zip. Thread a piece of ribbon through the pull tab and either knot it or work a couple of stitches to keep it in place.

Gather
- Fabric for bag: one piece 35cm x 35cm (13⅞in x 13⅞in)
- Fabric for lining: one piece 35cm x 35cm (13⅞in x 13⅞in)

- Fabric for bow: two pieces 11cm x 40cm (4⅜in x 15½in)
- Medium fusible interlining

- Blue sewing thread
- 20cm navy blue zip
- Decorative ribbon for loop and pull tab

Templates for this project can be found at the back of the book. Full-size templates are available at: http://ideas.sewandso.co.uk/patterns

LINDA CLEMENTS

Anniversary Pillow

This pretty cushion would make a lovely anniversary memento. The couple's initials can be embroidered into one of the hearts to personalize the gift.

2. Sew the two short borders to the patchwork and press seams outwards. Sew on the longer borders and press.

3. To quilt, copy the heart template onto card and cut out. Position within a triangle and lightly pencil around the shape. Repeat in all triangles, flipping the template on alternate triangles. For the border, make a paper copy of the template. Tape it to a bright window. Tape the patchwork on top, with the corner heart positioned at the corner. Trace the corner pattern lightly with a pencil. Now rotate the patchwork to trace the design into another corner, and so on. Safety pin the wadding to the back of the patchwork. Use six strands of dark pink thread to quilt the hearts on the patchwork and white thread to quilt the border design.

4. Put the backing right sides together with the front; sew 1.3cm (½in) from the edge, leaving an opening. Clip corners, turn through; press. Insert a 35.5cm (14in) pad; sew up the gap. Sew a button through the centre front and back.

Templates for this project can be found at the back of the book. Full-size templates are available at: http://ideas.sewandso.co.uk/patterns

1. To make half-square triangles, pin a pale square right sides together with a print square. Draw a line from corner to corner. Sew 6mm (¼in) on either side of the line. Cut along the line, open the two units and press seams. Repeat to make another two. Check that the units are 14cm (5½in) square. Arrange units in a windmill pattern and then sew them together.

Gather
- Fabric for patchwork: **two** 15.2cm (6in) squares of pale fabric; **two** 15.2cm (6in) squares of print fabric

- Dark pink fabric for borders/ backing: **two** strips 7.6cm x 26.7cm (3in x 10½in); **two** strips 7.6cm x 39.4cm (3in x 15½in); **one** 39.4cm (15½in) square

- Wadding (batting) 39.4cm (15½in) square
- Pink and white stranded cotton (floss)
- Two buttons
- 35.5cm (14in) cushion pad

ELLEN KHARADE

Slice of Fabric Cake

This fabric cake is a lasting reminder of a birthday celebration and can be used long after the event as a useful pincushion. Choose from two sweet designs.

1. Use the template to make patterns for the cake top, side, base and back. Place the cake top pattern on top of the foam, aligning one edge with the edge of the foam; draw around the shape and use a craft knife to cut along the marked lines.

2. Using the patterns, cut a cake top from patterned fabric, and cut two sides, one base and one back from white felt.

3. With right sides facing, pin the long side of the patterned fabric to the long side of one of the felt side pieces. Machine stitch in place. Now pin the other long side of the patterned fabric to the long side of the second felt side piece, and again machine stitch in place. Pin the felt back piece to the short side of the patterned fabric and machine stitch as before. Pin the side seams together, and once again machine stitch in place to complete the cover.

4. Pull the cover over the foam. Place the felt base beneath the foam; pin the seams and hand stitch. To hide the join, hand sew ric rac across the fabric change.

5. To decorate the cake slice, hand sew a length of ribbon round the edge making sure that it is centred; and embellish the top with pearl and seed beads, felt flowers and small pompoms cut in half.

Gather
- White felt
- Patterned fabric
- Pink felt flowers
- Pink ribbon and ric rac
- Small pompoms
- Green and pink pearl and seed beads
- Piece of foam 5cm (2in) deep

Templates for this project can be found at the back of the book. Full-size templates are available at: http://ideas.sewandso.co.uk/patterns

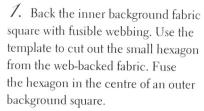

LINDA CLEMENTS

Harvest Fruit Coasters

These coasters, made in warm shades and decorated with easy blanket stitch appliqué, will suit most kitchen styles and make useful Thanksgiving gifts.

1. Back the inner background fabric square with fusible webbing. Use the template to cut out the small hexagon from the web-backed fabric. Fuse the hexagon in the centre of an outer background square.

2. Cut a 7.6cm (3in) square of green or yellow print for the apple or pear. Cut a 5cm (2in) square each of green fabric and dark green for leaf and stalk. Back the appliqué fabric squares with fusible webbing. Cut out the shapes. Peel off the papers and position the fruit, leaf and stalk on the hexagon; fuse into place.

3. Use three strands of embroidery thread to blanket stitch around the appliqués and the inner hexagon. Use backstitch for the leaf vein and outline the stalk.

4. Shape the background squares to the coaster shape using the large hexagon template. Cut wadding 6mm (¼in) smaller and pin to the back of the fronts. Pin fronts and backs together; sew 6mm (¼in) seam leaving a turning gap. Turn; press in open edges; topstitch close to edge.

Templates for this project can be found at the back of the book. Full-size templates are available at: http://ideas.sewandso.co.uk/patterns

---

Gather
- Outer background fabric: two 16.5cm (6½in) squares per coaster
- Inner background fabric: one 11.4cm (4½in) square per coaster

- Yellow print for pear appliqué or green print for apple appliqué
- Scraps of green fabrics for leaf and stalk appliqués

- Fusible webbing
- Wadding (batting)
- Dark brown stranded cotton (floss)

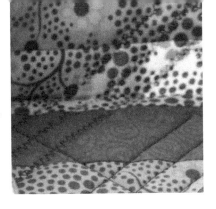

LINDA CLEMENTS

Patchwork Pocket Tidy

This fabric box makes a great Father's Day present, giving Dad somewhere to store his pocket contents tidily until morning.

1. Using 6mm (¼in) seams, sew the strips together, alternating the colours: dark, medium, light. Press seams. Cut the unit into two squares each 29.8cm (11¾in).

2. Safety pin the wadding to the back of one of the patchwork squares, leaving the seam allowance free. Pin the other square right sides together with the first square, aligning all edges. Sew together all round leaving a gap for turning.

3. Clip corners, turn through. Sew the gap up and press. With matching thread, topstitch round 3mm (⅛in) from the edge.

4. Quilt the patchwork using red quilting thread and any pattern you like.

5. Press all sides in by 5cm (2in), pressing firmly to crease the base. Take each corner in turn and pinch the two top edges together so the sides are vertical. Using matching thread, stitch through the two edges, 5cm (2in) in from each corner, to fix the corner. Press the flap of fabric inwards, to make a kite shape, and sew a button in position. Repeat on all four corners.

Gather

- Dark print fabric: three strips 4.4cm x 61cm (1¾in x 24in)
- Medium print fabric: three strips 4.4cm x 61cm (1¾in x 24in)
- Light print fabric: three strips 4.4cm x 61cm (1¾in x 24in)
- Wadding (batting) 28cm (11in) square
- Sewing threads and red quilting thread
- Four buttons

CAROL MAY

Ribbon Flower Fascinator

This ribbon flower accessory can be stitched onto a headband or onto a hair clip.
Alternatively, attach a safety pin for an impressive wedding corsage.

1. Take the black patterned ribbon and fold and pleat the ribbon petals one at a time, hand stitching as you go. Make five petals in a circle.

2. Take the red patterned ribbon and fold and pleat this on top of the first circle of ribbon petals, again making five petals in a circle.

3. Take thin white patterned ribbon and stitch a group of loops over the second circle of ribbon loops. You can cut the folds or leave uncut as you prefer.

4. Place the small button on top of the large button and sew in the centre of the ribbon flower. Sew the flower securely to the headband.

Gather
- Black, red and white patterned ribbons
- Large white button and small pink flower-shaped button
- Red sewing thread
- Headband

KIRSTY NEALE

Vintage Noticeboard

This decorative pinboard can be created from an old picture frame, with the glass removed and cork tiles or vintage fabric added in its place.

1. Carefully remove any glass from your frame and set aside. Sand the wooden edges of the frame. Brush or spray on two or three coats of paint.

2. Cover the frame backing with adhesive cork, or glue on cork tiles. If your frame doesn't have a back, cut a piece of mount board to fit, and cover this with cork instead.

3. Cut a piece of fabric to cover the cork backing, allowing an extra 5cm (2in) around all sides. Spray adhesive over the cork surface and place your fabric on top. Smooth out any wrinkles and fold the excess over the sides and stick to the back of the board.

4. Spread glue around the recess inside the edges of the frame. Press the fabric-covered board firmly into place behind the frame, and set aside to dry.

5. Glue vintage buttons to the top of your drawing pins to decorate.

Gather
- Vintage picture frame
- Sandpaper
- Spray paint or acrylic paint and paintbrush
- Adhesive cork or cork tiles
- Mount board (optional)
- Spray adhesive
- Vintage (or vintage-inspired) fabric
- Strong glue
- Drawing pins
- Vintage buttons

KIRSTY NEALE

Felt & Fabric Corsage

This simple, machine-stitched, corsage-style brooch is made from felt with vintage fabric, ribbon and buttons. It can be easily adapted into a hairclip.

1. Copy the flower template onto felt and cut out. Trace the four circle templates onto fusible webbing and iron each one onto the back of a piece of vintage fabric. Cut out the fabric circles, then peel away the backing paper.

2. Place the largest circle on top of the felt flower and iron into place. Add the remaining circles in the same way. Machine stitch over the top to secure, using a mixture of straight and zigzag stitch.

3. Sew two or three vintage buttons on top to decorate the front of the brooch. Cut two lengths of ribbon and glue to the back of the felt flower. Trim diagonally across the ends of each piece to stop them fraying.

4. Cut a circle of felt to cover the back of your brooch. Sew a brooch pin to the circle, roughly a third of the way down from the top edge.

5. Stick the felt circle firmly and neatly into place over the back of the brooch. Allow the glue to dry overnight before wearing.

Gather
- Felt
- Fusible web
- Scraps of vintage fabric
- Vintage buttons
- Vintage ribbon or trim
- Brooch pin
- Fabric glue

Templates for this project can be found at the back of the book. Full-size templates are available at: http://ideas.sewandso.co.uk/patterns

CLAIRE GARLAND

Polka Dot Pan Holder

A stylish and practical kitchen accessory, this polka dot pan holder is part sewn, part knitted and will cheer you as you cook.

1. **Knitted panel**

Tension (US: gauge): *15sts x 16.5 rows = 10cm (4in) in stocking stitch*

Md (make dot) – knit into front, knit into back, knit into front of next stitch (3sts yarn **CC** on RH needle) turn, p3 tog, turn, k1.

In **MC** – Cast on 30sts.

Work st st for 4 rows.

Row 5: MC – k2, [**CC** – md, **MC** – k5] 4 times, **CC** – md, **MC** – k3. Cut yarn **CC** at end of row.

St st 5 rows.

Row 11: [**MC** – k5, **CC** – md] 4 times, **CC** – md, **MC** – k6.

St st 5 rows.

Repeat last 12 rows (Rows 5–16) once.

Row 29: as row 5

End with 4 rows st st.

Cast off (bind off) k-wise.

Weave in stray ends.

2. Attach yarn **MC** and **CC** held together to one of the corners and work 16ch. Join with slip stitch in base of first ch. Weave in ends. If necessary lightly steam and re-shape into a square, using the felt square as a guide.

3. Using the felt square as a guide press a 1cm (³⁄₈in) hem all round the fabric square to wrong sides. Pin wrong sides together, then whip stitch the fabric to the knitted panel with the felt square sandwiched between.

Gather	• 1 x 50g (1¾oz) ball grey aran yarn (**MC**) • Small amounts DK yarn for the polka dots (**CC**)	• 7mm (US size 10½) knitting needles • 5.00mm (US size 8/H) crochet hook	• Vintage fabric 22 x 22cm (8½ x 8½in) • Wool felt 20 x 20cm (8 x 8in)	**Abbreviations used in knitting pattern**

Abbreviations used in knitting pattern

k knit

p3 tog purl 3 together (2 sts decreased)

p purl

st st stocking st (US: stockinette st) (alternate k&p rows)

st/s stitch/es

ELLEN KHARADE

Vintage-Print Quilted Make-up Bag

An elegant bag that features vintage-style fabric and quilted raw silk. It can be used as a make-up bag or as a clutch bag for an evening event.

1. Back the floral and silk fabrics with interfacing. Pin the templates for the bag front, back and flap to the floral fabric and cut out the pieces. Pin the templates for the flap to the

silk and wadding and cut out. Cut a back and a front from lining fabric.

2. Pin the wadding to the silk wrong side and tack around the

shape to hold it together. On the front, machine stitch vertical lines 2cm (¾in) apart in a lighter thread.

3. Lay the patterned flap on top of patterned bag front, wrong sides together. Mark washer position for clasp. Make a slit in the marks through both fabrics. From right side push clasps through slits in the front piece and fold down prongs. Attach the other part of clasp to flap.

4. With right sides facing, place quilted flap and floral flap together. Machine stitch round curve. With right sides facing, pin lining pieces together and stitch round sides and base, leaving 10cm (4in) gap in base. With right sides facing, pin floral back and front together and stitch sides and base. Pin flap to back of bag, right outside of flap against right outside of bag back. Tack all layers, with raw edges even.

5. With right sides facing insert bag into lining. Pin all thicknesses together and stitch. Turn out through opening and arrange lining. Slip stitch the gap.

6. Make a yo-yo and sew it and the button to the bag front.

Gather

- Floral cotton fabric 35 x 45cm (14 x 18in)
- Jade silk 35 x 45cm (14 x 18in)
- Lightweight iron-on

interfacing 70 x 90cm (28 x 36in)
- Wadding (batting)
- Coordinating lining fabric

- Yo-yo fabric 11cm (4½in) circle
- Vintage button
- Thin brass-toned clasp 14cm (5½in)

Templates for this project can be found at the back of the book. Full-size templates are available at: http://ideas.sewandso.co.uk/patterns

KIRSTY NEALE

Pretty Faux Enamel Flower Pins

This flower brooch is made from layers of shrink plastic with curved petals to echo the look of mid-century enamel brooches.

1. Use the templates to trace and then cut out one small and one or two large flowers from shrink plastic, depending on whether you want to make a two- or three-layer brooch.

2. Colour both sides of the plastic with permanent marker pens. You can either use a single shade, or blend two together for a different look. Don't worry if the ink looks streaky – this just adds to the finished effect and looks more natural.

3. Take the small flower and shrink it, using a heat gun or by placing it in the oven. While the plastic is still warm, carefully pick it up and curve the petals gently around a large wooden bead.

4. Heat the large flower(s) in the same way, but instead of using a bead, shape the petals around the smaller flower.

5. Stick the flowers together, one inside the other. Add seed beads, a gem or button to the centre. Glue a brooch pin to the back of the finished flower.

Gather
- White shrink plastic
- Permanent marker pens
- Heat gun (or oven)
- Large wooden bead
- Seed beads, gems or fancy buttons
- Brooch pin
- Strong glue

Templates for this project can be found at the back of the book. Full-size templates are available at: http://ideas.sewandso.co.uk/patterns

ZOE LARKINS

Cat Pincushion Bracelet

Here's a little gift that's quite literally the cat's whiskers! Feline fun for a young sewer who's also mad about kitties.

1. Using the template, cut out two cat head shapes from the patterned fabric. Use the felt to make a face on one of the head shapes: cut two circles of white felt for the cheeks, a little pink heart for the nose, and a sandstone triangle for the forehead/ bridge of the nose.

2. Use white thread and slip stitch to sew on the felt face.

3. Sew on the two large mother-of-pearl buttons with black thread for the cat's eyes.

4. Pin the two head shapes together, with right sides facing. Machine stitch all the way round the edge with a 6mm (¼in) seam allowance, leaving a small gap at the bottom for turning. Stuff the head and neatly stitch the gap closed.

5. Cut a piece of elastic to fit your wrist, and thread beads on to make a bracelet. Stitch the bracelet onto the back of the head. Wear your pincushion bracelet as you sew, sticking your pins into your cat's cheeks to look like whiskers!

Gather
- Scraps of fabric for pincushion
- White, pink and sandstone felt
- Two large mother-of-pearl buttons
- White and black sewing thread
- Thick elastic cord
- Beads
- Toy filling

Templates for this project can be found at the back of the book.
Full-size templates are available at:
http://ideas.sewandso.co.uk/patterns

JANE MILLARD

Felt Rose Corsage

Felt comes in such intense colours that are perfect for creating this stunning floral adornment. As a present to the bride offer to supply all of the corsages.

1. Cut a 15cm (6in) diameter pink felt circle and cut into a spiral.

2. Roll up the spiral from the outside edge to form the flower; keep the centre tight and loosen near the end to create a rose. Stitch the end to secure beneath the flower.

3. Cut two leaves and backstitch round the edges and through the centre with light green sewing thread for the veins.

4. Secure the leaves under the flower with a few neat stitches.

5. Cut a small circle of pink felt to cover the raw edges at the back of the flower and stitch in place. Stitch the finished rose onto the brooch back.

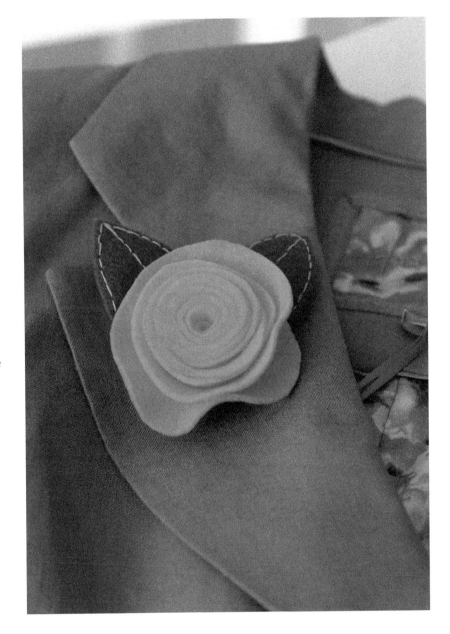

Gather
- Pink and green felt
- Light green sewing thread
- Brooch back

Needle Know-how

Hand stitching

Choose a needle that matches the thickness of your thread and that passes easily through the fabric without making unsightly holes. Stitches can be started with a knot on the back of your work and finished off neatly at the back, with a backstitch.

Backstitch	Blanket stitch	Chain stitch	Cross stitch
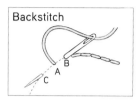	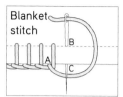	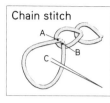	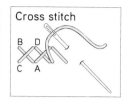

French knot	Hem stitch	Ladder stitch	Running stitch
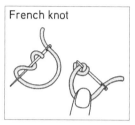	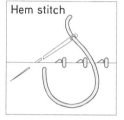	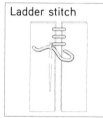	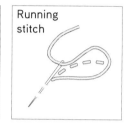

Satin stitch	Slip stitch	Topstitch	Whip stitch (oversewing)
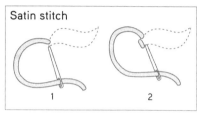			

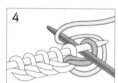

Knit

Please note that knitting patterns in this book use UK terminology. Where necessary the US equivalent is given on the individual project pages and here, in the caption to the illustration.

cast on

1	2	3	4
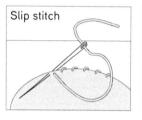	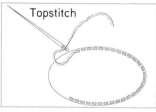		

knit 2 stitches together

make 1 stitch (to the left)

1	2	3
	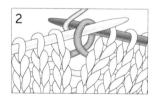	

purl 2 stitches together

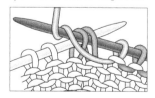

make 1 stitch (to the right)

1	2	3
	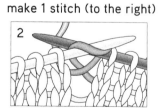	

knit into front and back of stitch

cast off (US: bind off)

1	2	3
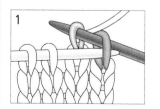		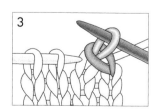

Both the 'English' style of knitting (with the yarn held in the right hand) and the 'continental' style (with the yarn held in the left hand) are shown here. The 'continental' style is considered to be a quicker, more efficient way of working. Try out both styles to see which suits you best.

knit stitch (English)

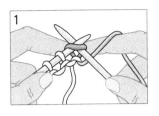 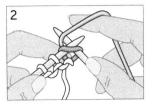 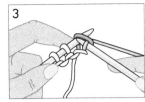 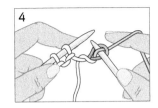

purl stitch (English)

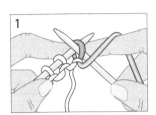 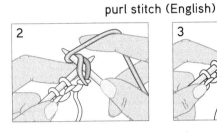 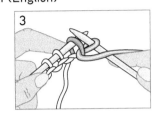 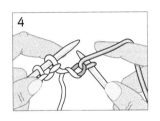

knit stitch (continental)

 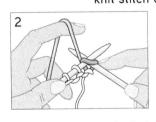 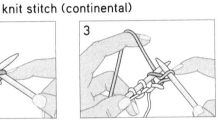 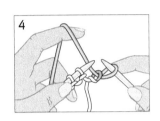

purl stitch (continental)

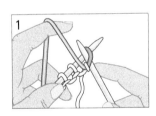 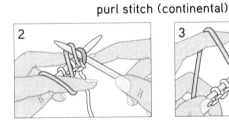 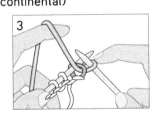 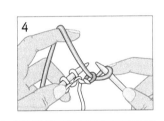

Crochet

Please note that crochet patterns in this book use UK terminology. Where necessary the US equivalent is indicated in the Abbreviations given on the individual project pages and here, in the captions to the illustrations.

slip knot

slip stitch

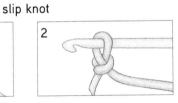

chain

double crochet (US: single crochet)

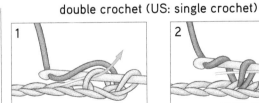 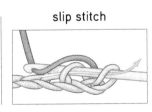

treble (US: double crochet)

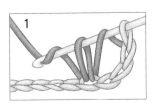 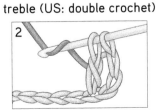 

Templates

IMPORTANT: all templates shown at 50% of original size. Enlarge to 200% to give full size template. Full-size templates are available at: http://ideas.sewandso.co.uk/patterns.

Bird mp3 Player Case

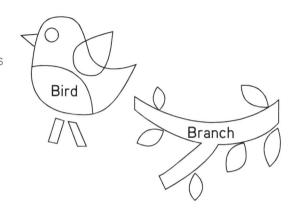

Hanging Fabric Hearts

Cat Pincushion Bracelet

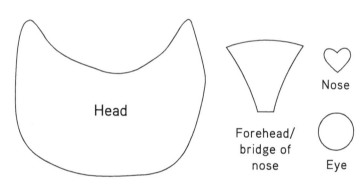

Retro Mobile Case

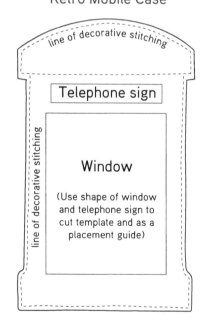

Felt & Fabric Corsage

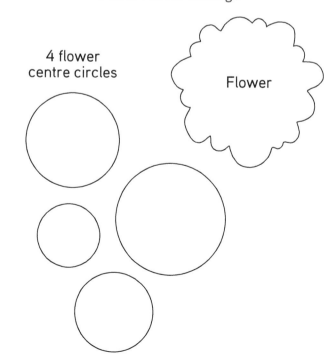

Vintage Paper Bracelet

3D Paper Hearts

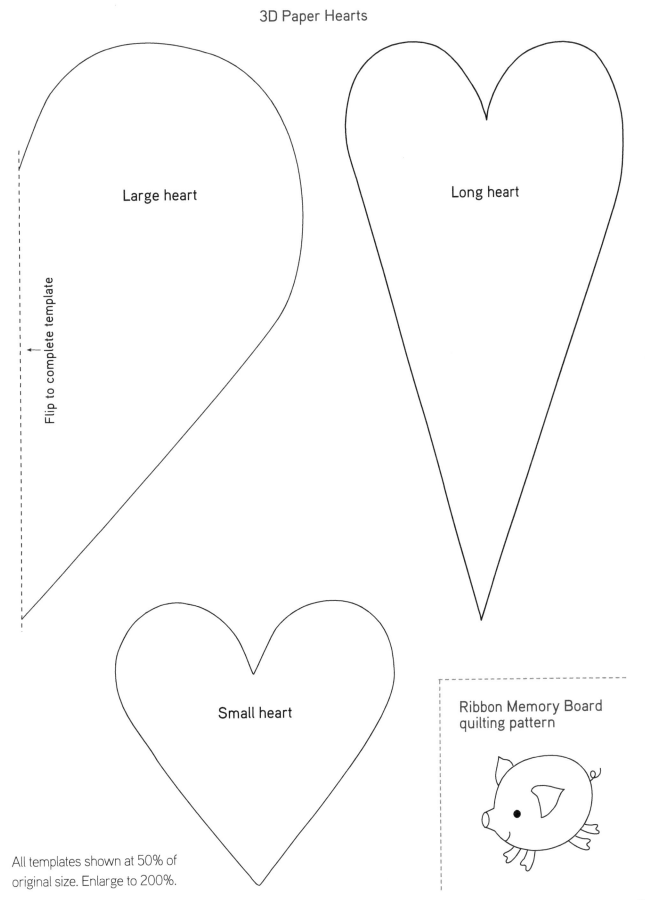

Large heart

Flip to complete template

Long heart

Small heart

Ribbon Memory Board
quilting pattern

All templates shown at 50% of
original size. Enlarge to 200%.

Cottage Tea Cosy

All templates shown at 50% of original size. Enlarge to 200%.

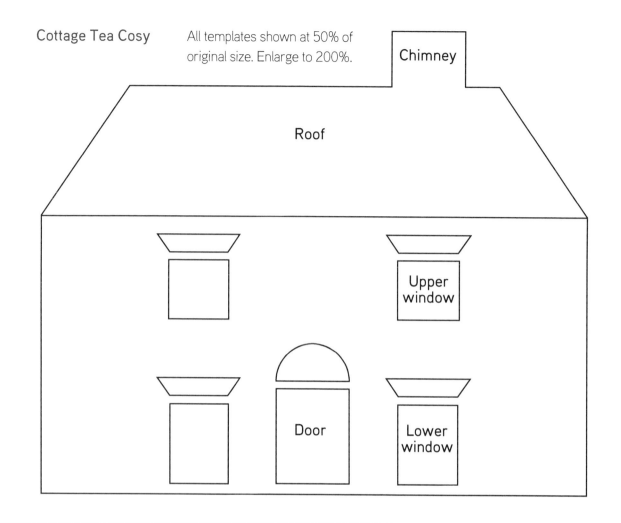

Chimney

Roof

Upper window

Door

Lower window

Cute Egg Cosies

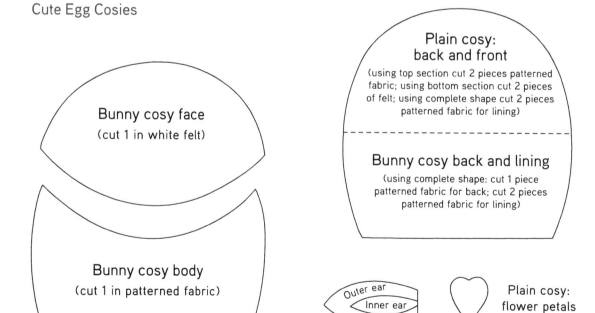

Bunny cosy face
(cut 1 in white felt)

Bunny cosy body
(cut 1 in patterned fabric)

Plain cosy:
back and front
(using top section cut 2 pieces patterned fabric; using bottom section cut 2 pieces of felt; using complete shape cut 2 pieces patterned fabric for lining)

Bunny cosy back and lining
(using complete shape: cut 1 piece patterned fabric for back; cut 2 pieces patterned fabric for lining)

Outer ear
Inner ear

Plain cosy:
flower petals
(cut 5 in felt)

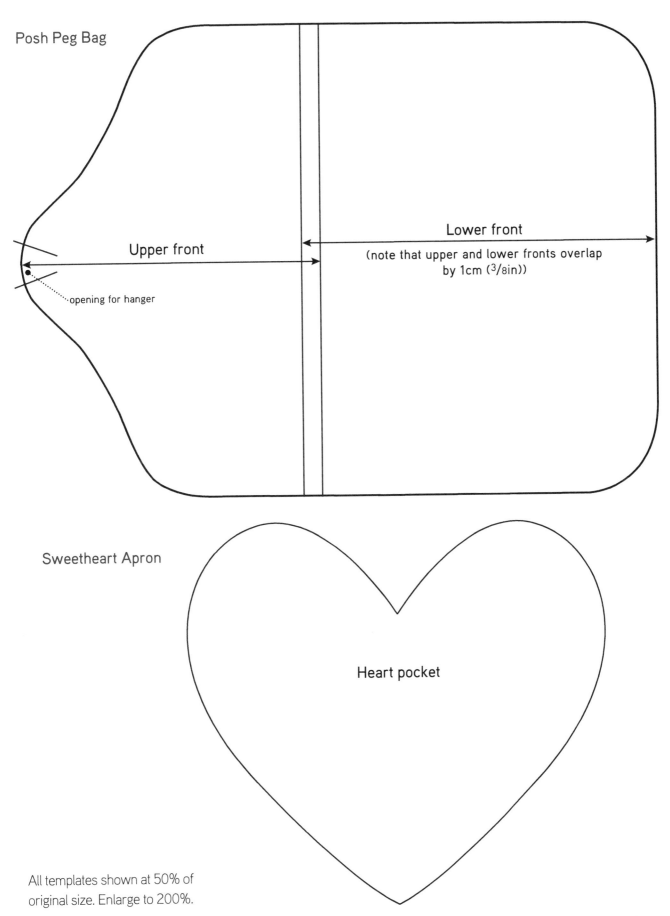

Posh Peg Bag

Upper front

Lower front
(note that upper and lower fronts overlap
by 1cm (3/8in))

opening for hanger

Sweetheart Apron

Heart pocket

All templates shown at 50% of
original size. Enlarge to 200%.

Retro Curtain Bag
Use the full template to cut the lining

Slice of Fabric Cake

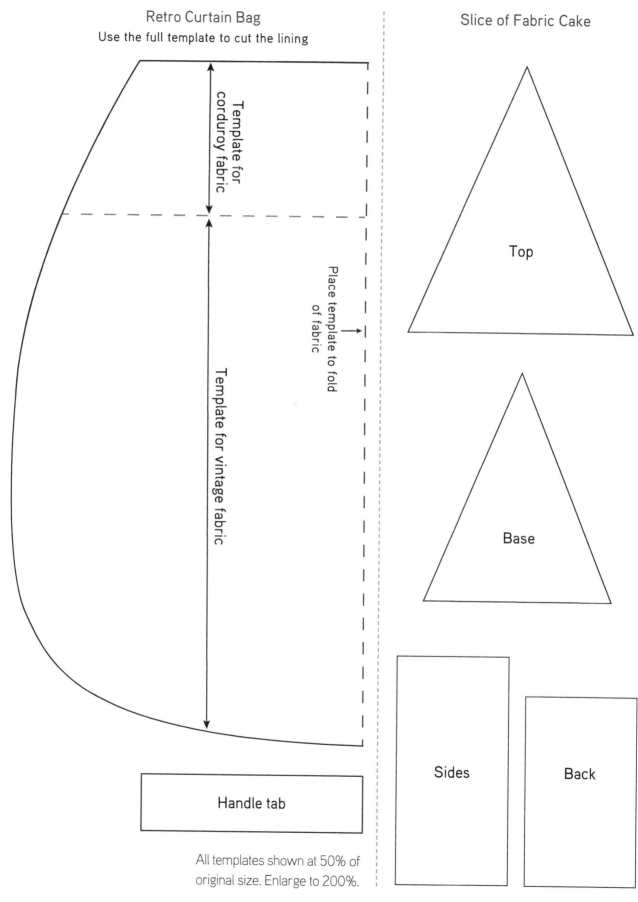

Template for corduroy fabric

Place template to fold of fabric

Template for vintage fabric

Handle tab

Top

Base

Sides

Back

All templates shown at 50% of original size. Enlarge to 200%.

Coffee Pot Cosy

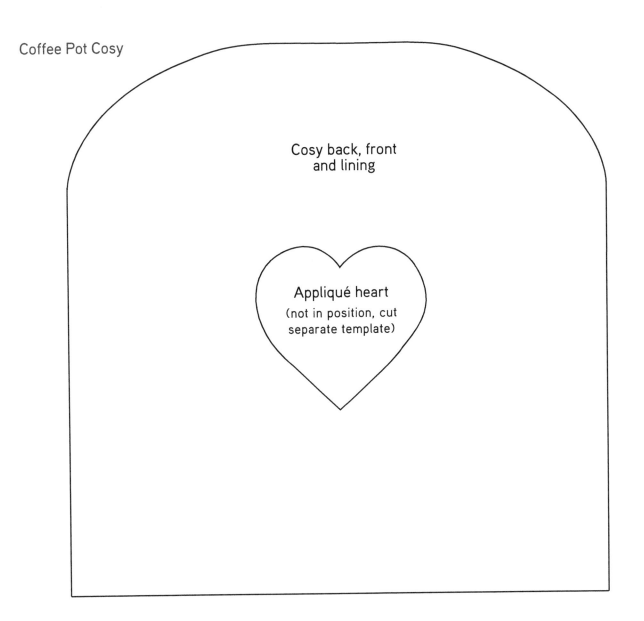

Cosy back, front
and lining

Appliqué heart
(not in position, cut
separate template)

Harvest Coasters

All templates shown at 50% of
original size. Enlarge to 200%.

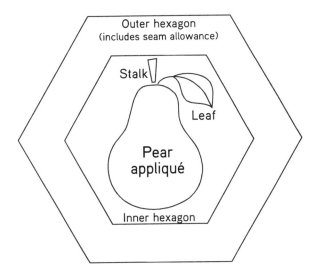

Outer hexagon
(includes seam allowance)

Stalk

Leaf

Pear
appliqué

Inner hexagon

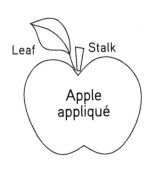

Leaf   Stalk

Apple
appliqué

Vintage-Print Quilted Make-up Bag

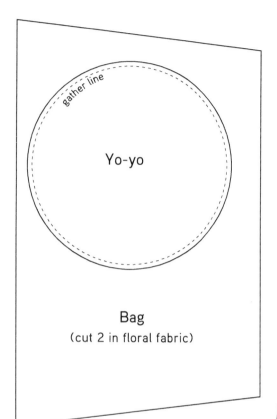

gather line

Yo-yo

Bag
(cut 2 in floral fabric)

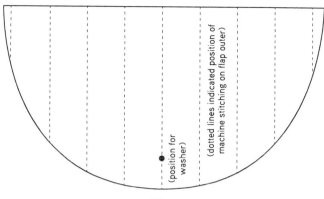

(position for washer)

(dotted lines indicated position of machine stitching on flap outer)

Flap
(cut 1 in silk for outer flap; cut 1 in floral fabric for
lining flap; cut 2 in wadding)

Lining
(cut 2 in lining fabric)

Anniversary Pillow quilting pattern

To help align the templates,
the blue lines indicate the
positon of one of the
half-square triangles

Patchwork Coasters quilting pattern

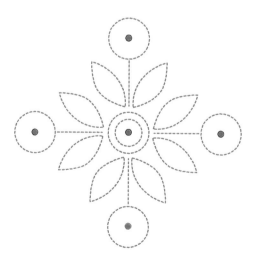

All templates shown at 50% of
original size. Enlarge to 200%.

Bow Make-up Purse

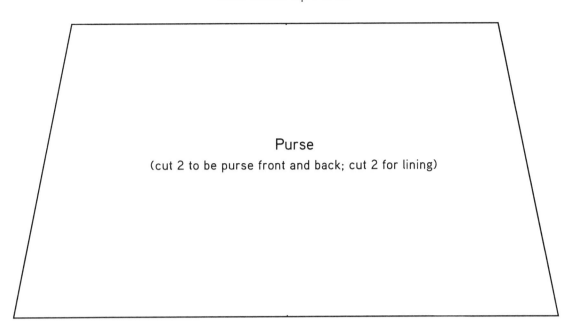

Purse
(cut 2 to be purse front and back; cut 2 for lining)

Pretty Faux Enamel Flower Pins

Flower design 1

Flower design 2

All templates shown at 50% of
original size. Enlarge to 200%.

A SEWANDSO BOOK
© F&W Media International, Ltd 2016

SewandSo is an imprint of F&W Media International, Ltd
Pynes Hill Court, Pynes Hill, Exeter EX2 5AZ, UK

F&W Media International, Ltd is a subsidiary of F+W Media, Inc
10151 Carver Road, Suite #200, Blue Ash, OH 45242, USA

Text and Designs © F&W Media International, Ltd 2016
Layout, photography and illustrations © F&W Media International, Ltd 2016

First published in the UK and USA in 2016
Content previously published in: *101 Ways to Stitch, Craft, Create* (2012); *101 Ways to Stitch, Craft, Create for All Occasions* (2013); *101 Ways to Stitch, Craft, Create Vintage* (2013); and *101 Easy to Make Craft Projects* (2013).

A catalogue record for this book is available from the British Library.

ISBN-13: 978-1-4463-0662-8 paperback
SRN: R5809 paperback

ISBN-13: 978-1-4463-7551-8 PDF
SRN: R5257 PDF

ISBN-13: 978-1-4463-7550-1 ePUB
SRN: R5258 ePUB

Content Director: Ame Verso
Senior Editor: Jeni Hennah
Design Manager: Anna Wade
Photographers: Sian Irvine and Jack Gorman
Project Editor/Layout: Sue Cleave
Production Manager: Beverley Richardson

Layout of the digital edition of this book may vary depending on reader hardware and display settings.

F+W Media publishes high quality books on a wide range of subjects.
For more great book ideas visit **www.sewandso.co.uk**

Lightning Source UK Ltd.
Milton Keynes UK
UKHW05f0331160218

317990UK00001B/16/P

9 781446 306628